Forgotten Ireland

scenes from the 19th century camera

Forgotten Ireland

scenes from the 19th century camera

Martin Howard

GRAMERCY

This 2000 edition is published by Gramercy Books™,
an imprint of Random House Value Publishing, Inc.,
201 East 50th Street, New York, New York, 10022.
by arrangement with PRC Publishing Ltd, London.

Gramercy Books™ and design are registered trademarks of
Random House Value Publishing, Inc.
Random House
New York • Toronto • London • Sydney • Auckland
http://www.randomhouse.com/

A CIP catalogue record for this book is available from the Library of
Congress.

ISBN 0-517-16159-1

8 7 6 5 4 3 2 1
Printed and bound in China

All the pictures in this book have been kindly supplied from the Lawrence
Collection by the National Library of Ireland, with the exception of the fol-
lowing:
Pages 6 (both), 33 and 63 courtesy of Bord Failte - Irish Tourist Board;
Page 8 reproduced by courtesy of the Public Record Office. Crown
Copyright material in the Public Record Office is reproduced by permission
of the Controller of Her Majesty's Stationary Office.

Page 2: The typical 19th century cottage was a basic but cozy dwelling.

CONTENTS

LISTOWEL ROSCOMMON TRIPPERARY DOWNPATRICK NEWTOWNARDS BUNCRANA BALLYSHANNON
KELLS TRIM NAAS DUBLIN BRAY GALWAY ATHLONE LONGFORD BELFAST LONDONDERRY
DUNDALK CORK WATERFORD CARLOW WEXFORD KILKENNY LIMERICK COLERAINE BALLYMENA
MONASTERY GLENCAR SLIEVEARDAGH HILLS LOUGH ENNELL BANTRY BAY GIANT'S CAUSEWAY
CARPET-MAKING FURNITURE CLOTHING COBBLING TOURISM LACE-MAKING EMBROIDERY BOAT
O'QUIRKE O'CONNELL DILLON O'FLANAGAN O'DEVLIN O'KENNY O'GRADY O'SHEA NUGENT

INTRODUCTION

Ireland today is the success story of Europe and the prosperity of the capital city, Dublin, reflects that of the rest of the country. A walk through St. Stephen's Green, where office workers enjoy lunch and the sun during summer, down the gentle slope of busy Grafton Street to O'Connell Street and the River Liffey reveals a vital, dynamic city. World-class hotels jostle for space with the trappings of a financial renaissance—smart restaurants offering haute cuisine, hi-tech banks, cyber-cafés, and high street shops selling designer clothes and expensive jewelry. Further along the quay, past the Ha'penny Bridge and turning left into Temple Bar, is the thriving cultural and social heart of the city. The Film Institute, theater schools, and galleries are interspersed with pubs where musicians play day and night. Artists, actors, and bohemians mix with the tourists who throng the busy streets here, drinking coffee outside the fashionable patisseries while watching the street artists.

Signs of Irish success are apparent outside Dublin as well. Investment from overseas—notably from the world's biggest computer companies—the success of home-grown businesses, and a thriving tourist industry have made the Ireland of the 21st century more prosperous than at any other time in its history. And with the peace process in Northern Ireland continuing to make progress, it is to be hoped that the future may also bring lasting harmony to the whole island after a long period of strife and unrest.

Left: This Connemara weaver looks as if he has been weaving wool for centuries.

Right: The typical 19th century cottage was a basic but cozy dwelling. The center of the house would have been the hearth where cooking took place, water was heated for baths and laundry, and the family huddled for warmth on cold winter nights.

IRELAND DURING the 19th CENTURY

Beneath the surface of today's prosperity lies a very different nation—the contrast of modern Ireland with Ireland of the 19th century could not be starker. The bloody rebellion of 1798, fomented by the United Irishmen under Wolfe Tone and supported by French forces, led a British government to the Act of Union in 1801; the Irish Parliament was dissolved and the British took control. For the remainder of the century and for the first decades of the next, the country was a stew of political and religious tension. The additional hardship of extreme famine saw millions of people leaving their homeland, destined for a better life across the Atlantic.

Although the divisions between rich and poor were extreme throughout 19th century Europe, in Ireland they were especially severe. The Industrial Revolution taking place in Britain almost completely passed Ireland by. With the exception of Belfast, Ireland remained a largely agricultural country, the main crop being potatoes. Land was generally owned by the Protestant aristocracy, many of who were British absentee landlords; rents for the tenant farmers were exorbitant and, due to a high population of 8.5 million before the famine, the plots of land available were small. Farmers enjoyed no fixed tenure and, as happened more and more often during the years of famine, could be evicted from their land and homes at any time. In addition, the aristocratic Protestants—heavily influenced by the anti-Catholic Orange Order—also controlled the local administration and saw to it that the Catholic population was firmly under their heel. A further injustice, particularly galling for a population that was 80 per cent Catholic, was that the Protestant Church of Ireland expected to be paid a tithe.

This was the background against which was set a century of struggle and hardship as Ireland toiled toward freedom. The early decades of the 19th century saw Daniel O'Connell (1775–1847), a brilliant lawyer from County Kerry who would be

Far left: Ireland in 1804. Described as a "New Map of Ireland. . . for the use of Travellers," this map was compiled originally by Alexander Taylor, a Lieutenant in the Royal Engineers. Although a commercially produced map, it is of considerable interest for the alterations made in manuscript pointing out the defensive arrangements around the coast. A key, at the top right, describes in detail the various military establishments—both actual and proposed—demonstrating the considerable importance that was attached to the defense of Ireland at a time of threat from the French forces under Napoleon. When the map was compiled, it was only a few years since the French had supported an attempted rebellion by Irish nationalists. So the threat that these defensive stations were designed to counter was very real.

Left: Guards on parade at Dublin Castle, the bastion of British rule in Ireland. This building became so closely associated with the government in the popular mind that "the Castle" became a universal synonym for the British administration in Ireland.

called the "Liberator," mobilizing the oppressed Catholics into a peaceful political force. He was backed by a formidably large portion of the population, who took part in huge, peaceful demonstrations. O'Connell eventually managed to bring the British government, led by the Duke of Wellington, to pass the Catholic Relief Bill which extended the same rights to the Catholic population as those enjoyed by the Protestants. However, the government simultaneously raised the property qualification needed to vote from 40 shillings to £10, which effectively destroyed O'Connell's electoral base. The great politician, after whom Dublin's famous O'Connell Street was named, spent the rest of his days struggling to repeal the Act of Union.

A country where one crop is grown to the exclusion of others is always vulnerable to famine if that crop fails, and in Ireland a bad potato harvest often brought years of poverty and malnutrition. But because the potato gives a relatively large and nutritious crop from a small acreage, farmers had no choice. If they grew wheat, they would certainly not have had enough to feed their family through even a fraction of the winter—even if the harvest was bountiful. So when a potato blight reached Ireland in 1845, the effects were predictably devastating. At the time almost two million peasants were already struggling to survive and even a relatively rapid response from the British Tory government had little effect in relieving the misery. The British prime minister of the time, Robert Peel, commissioned scientists to find the cause of the blight and also brought 100,000 tons of maize from America to be sold at low prices from special distribution depots. Nevertheless, given that the worst affected people had no money at all, relief was limited and the Irish poor suffered dreadful privations. Over the next few years many simply died on the road while searching for food. In July 1847 the *Dublin University Magazine* published the "Song of the Famine," which paints a bleak and powerful portrait of the sufferings:

Right: Cottage industries such as lace-making and embroidery helped impoverished women to earn money for food though shoes for everyday use would have been a luxury. The great lace-making centers of Ireland were traditionally Carrickmacross and Limerick.

Food! Food! Food!
Beware before you spurn,
Ere the cravings of the famishing
To loathing madness turn;
For hunger is a fearful spell,
And fearful work is done,
Where the key to many a reeking crime,
Is the curse of living on!

Home! Home! Home!
A dreary fireless hole
A miry floor and a dripping roof,
And a little straw—its whole.
Only the ashes that smoulder not,
Their blaze was long ago,
And the empty space for kettle and pot,
Where once they stood in a row.

WATER CARRIER . 2916. W. L.

With the exception of 1847, when a small crop was harvested from a much-reduced store of seed potatoes, the crisis lasted until 1849. During this time the majority of Irish people had to rely on the diminishing charity of the British government, that attempted to institute similar poverty measures to those taken in England. Thus workhouses started to appear and people who were so hungry that they were barely able to stand were forced into long hours of arduous work to earn a pitiful meal. The eventual cost of the Great Famine to Ireland was two million people—about half of whom starved to death while the other half emigrated, mostly for America. Despite better harvests after 1850, the flood of emigrants continued throughout the remainder of the century and by 1900 the population of Ireland had been reduced by almost half to about 4.25 million. Most of those who stayed remained unaffected by the fact that there was now more land to go round. A number of factors, including an agricultural move toward raising cattle and the passing of many holdings into the hands of financial speculators, ensured that evictions continued to be a common sight in rural Ireland, and many families struggled to find enough to eat.

This terrible situation galvanized politics in Ireland and where O'Connell had previously promoted constitutional and peaceful action to better the lot of the Irish poor, the new generation of activists espoused more militant tactics. The "Young Ireland" movement staged an uprising in 1848, which was so ineffective that it has become known as the "Battle of Widow McCormack's Cabbage Patch." Quickly put down by the British military, the leaders were transported to Tasmania. Nevertheless, militant political action continued apace, with the cause being taken up by the Fenian movement, kindled by emigrants in America and carried back to Ireland. Led by James Stephens (1824–1901) and John O'Mahony (1819–77), the Fenians organized a secret society called the Irish Republican

Page 12: For the poorest families or the victims of eviction, houses built of turf were often the answer. These primitive dwellings would be damp and dark as windows could not be cut from the walls. It would also have been difficult to construct an effective chimney so the "house" would usually be full of choking smoke.

Left: For a small remuneration the water carrier would take water from the local stream to those houses nearby that did not have access to a well or a pump.

Brotherhood or IRB, which was pledged to armed revolution. While the IRB's single armed uprising in 1867 disintegrated almost as soon as it started, the rescue of captured members in Britain provoked widespread support at home when three Fenians were executed after a British policeman was shot. Although the three had been at the scene of the rescue, none had fired the fatal shot and so British injustice created the "Manchester Martyrs." An explosion during a further attempted rescue at Clerkenwell prison in London killed a number of British civilians who lived close to the jail, and the outrage fired Gladstone's government to take the Irish situation much more seriously. Although their actions were curtailed, the secretive brotherhood remained intact and influential, gathering greater power that would erupt in the following generation.

In 1879 politics took a more peaceful turn when the Land League was founded with the aim of bringing an end to the evictions and winning the farmers tenancy rights over the land they worked. Two years later they had succeeded in securing the passage of the Land Act through the British parliament. This important bill asserted the "Three F's" for the Irish farmer—fair rents, fixity of tenure, and freedom for the tenant to sell his right of occupancy. This was an important milestone for Irish politics and a major boon to the many farmers who saw the power of their landlords crumble.

The year 1879 also saw the passionate and masterful politician Charles Stewart Parnell (1846–91) assume control of the Home Rule Party in the British parliament. A Protestant and a landlord, Parnell nevertheless adopted the Land League's policies and over the following years he gradually built up enormous popular support in Ireland, and a political party with 86 members. A champion of the tenant farmers, at the height of the evictions, Parnell declared:

"When a man takes a farm from which another has been evicted, you must show him . . . by leaving him severely alone, by putting him into a moral Coventry, by isolating him from his kind as if he were a leper of old—you must show him your detestation of the crimes he has committed."

A new verb—to "boycott"—would enter the English language as a result of the ostracization in 1880 of Captain C. Boycott, who was guilty of evicting tenants on his estates.

By 1886 Parnell had pushed Gladstone to introduce the first Home Rule Bill. This was defeated by a small majority, but Parnell's political aspirations—and the cohesion of the Home Rule Party—were destroyed when his affair with Kitty O'Shea led to a very public divorce case. He died prematurely but will be remembered, along with O'Connell, as one of 19th century Ireland's greatest politicians.

As the century drew to a close, the foundations were in place for independence from Britain. However, it would take a major uprising and a further two decades before a treaty was signed that would give Ireland her independence; and even then Northern Ireland remained under British rule—the ramifications of which are apparent to this day.

It is easy to think of history as a set of dates and political events and to pigeonhole the people. But not all the native Catholic people were starving to death and not all the landlords were heartless Protestant brutes who evicted their tenants without a second thought. Some cared deeply about the people that farmed the land and helped to clothe and feed their fellows during the famine. In 19th century Ireland, as elsewhere, and in every age, most of the people were more absorbed by their everyday lives and in making ends meet than they were in the machinations of their political masters. Some were more successful than others. The inhabitants of coastal towns continued to fill

Left: A scene that could never be repeated in the days of state pensions and central heating. Labor was the only asset that the 19th century Irish peasant possessed and even the elderly were expected to work to help keep the family. In this case an old woman emerges from the forest carrying wood that would probably have been used for kindling as peat was far less rare and used as fuel by all but the most wealthy who could afford the inflated prices of imported coal.

their plates from the sea, and some city dwellers scraped a living from trade and business; in the countryside others built makeshift huts from peat and existed on meager charity.

Culturally, the growth of nationalist feeling as the century progressed sparked a resurgence of Irish pride in the unique heritage and the 19th century saw a flowering of literature and traditional music. By the end of the century figures such as Oscar Wilde (1856–1900) and W.B. Yeats (1865–1939), themselves inspired by earlier 19th century writers such as Thomas Moore (1779–1852), had opened the door for Irish writers who proceeded to pen some of the greatest works of the modern literature. And writing was not the only area which found renewed interest. By the end of the century Irish sport, design, dance, and art were all flourishing.

the LAWRENCE LEGACY

On May 20, 1865, Ireland was at peace. The ravages of the Great Famine were over and the terrible memories beginning to fade, the short-lived Fenian uprising that would spark great changes in the Irish constitution was yet to ignite, and Parnell was yet to take his seat in British parliament. It was an uneventful day like many before it, and the opening of a photographic studio in Dublin opposite the General Post Office in Sackville Street (originally Drogheda Street, it has since been renamed O'Connell Street) went almost unnoticed. The shop of Mr. William Lawrence, however, would eventually bequeath to future generations some 40,000 glass plate negatives that constitute one of the biggest collections of photographs from that era anywhere in the world.

The principal photographer was Robert French, an ex-policeman who was initially employed by Lawrence as a printer. He later became a fully fledged, and very talented, photographer and over 30 years produced in excess of 30,000 photographs documenting every aspect of Irish life. Under the direction of his employer, French traveled the length and breadth of the Emerald Isle with his camera, taking pictures of cities and towns, rural cottages and landscapes, rich and poor alike. Showing the Irish at work, at home, and at play, these windows into history have provided us with an unparalleled view of a life and culture that has now all but vanished.

It was long assumed that the photographs were taken by Lawrence himself, as each of the negatives is carefully marked with his initials. However, as a busy Victorian businessman, and a typical member of the upper middle class, Lawrence would never have lowered himself to the position of artisan. And besides, he only had one arm, which would have made it impossible to carry around the heavy equipment needed to take a photograph in those days. It would be easy to assume, instead, that Lawrence exploited French's talents, as the latter is never credited for any of

Left: O'Connell Bridge, Dublin. this is a relatively early Lawrence photograph— horses and carts predominate and there are no motor cars to be seen. Lawrence was extremely keen that all of his scenes remain up-to-date and it was not unusual for French to take the same photograph many times. This has provided historians with an invaluable tool in seeing exactly how the towns changed over the final three and a half decades of the 19th century.

Left: The best of French's scenes are redolent of the time that they were taken. The smell of the horses and the cries of street vendors in this evocative picture of Ellison Street, Castlebar. The county town of Mayo, Castlebar was where the English cavalry were beaten in 1798 by French revolutionary soldiers and Irish peasants who were led by General Humbert.

Overleaf: Kinsale is an old and extremely pretty fishing town in West Cork and has been linked closely to the sea from its earliest days. Indeed it is said that one Alexander Selkirk, a traveler who departed the town in the 18th century, was the inspiration for Daniel Defoe's *Robinson Crusoe*, having been stranded for many years on a desert island after his ship was wrecked. The men in the photograph are curing the fish (the process of drying, salting, or smoking) so that they could be stored and transported to inland regions or exported.

his work, but the business relationship between the two men seems to have been one of mutual respect. French was allowed completely free rein when out in the field, a sign of great trust during this era, and a photograph that French took of his own parlor toward the end of his career shows a portrait of the Lawrence family hanging on the wall. It seems that French was quite content to be the unrecognized and stoic craftsman while his employer reaped the rewards of his artistry.

Lawrence's was just one of about 100 photographic studios that traded in Ireland in the 19th century (over 30 of which were established in Dublin). Following the invention of the camera in the early part of the century, public interest in the technological marvel remained high and the fashionable would visit studios again and again to have their portraits taken. Situated above a toyshop that was itself just a part of Lawrence's large emporium, the studio was to become Ireland's most successful. In its infancy it was noted for taking excellent portraits of Irish luminaries and celebrities passing through, but as time passed fads and fashions changed, and public interest turned from portraits to landscapes. As it became apparent that there was profit to be made out-doors, the forward-thinking Lawrence sent French out of Dublin on increasingly regular and longer assignments. They provided more and more material for the many souvenir albums and picture postcards of Irish scenes and the countryside for which the company would become famous. Keen that the photographs remain up-to-date, French returned to take many of the same scenes again and again. His shots are testament to the rapid progress of technology as the century reached its end: in the cities and towns, for example, trams, buses, and automobiles begin to take the place of horses and carts. Meanwhile, back in Sackville Street, other photographers busied themselves with portrait work. At its height the company employed somewhere in the region of fifty photographers, assistants, and colorists, and

also had a printing works out in the Dublin suburb of Rathmines. It was an extremely profitable business right up until the end, when two blows fell almost spontaneously. The first was the invention of the Box Brownie, which became instantly successful and gave everyone the ability to take their own photographs. Suddenly, the market that Lawrence had monopolized for so many years was open to anyone who could afford one of these relatively cheap cameras and his market began to dwindle

alarmingly. The second death-knell for Lawrence's photographic empire was the uprising of Easter Monday 1916, during which the insurgents barricaded themselves into the General Post Office opposite his shop. The following day, the slum dwellers who lived close by began to loot the parade of shops and Lawrence's was one of the first to be targeted, filled as it was with fancy goods and expensive photographic equipment. Subsequent shelling of the area by the army reduced the shop to smoking rubble and, tragically, the many decades worth of portrait photography—which included just about every famous person of the era to have ever set foot in Ireland—were stored within. More fortunately, the landscapes had been stored elsewhere and escaped destruction.

Soon after this the remaining photographs were sold at auction to the National Library of Ireland for £300. They remained in the vaults of the library virtually unnoticed until relatively recently, but have now been catalogued, transferred to microfilm, and are available for the public to view at the Gallery of Photography in Temple Bar, Dublin. Many other collections of the time were not so lucky, which is why the Lawrence collection is so important today. It remains one of the few comprehensive documents of a bygone age as well as a monument to the artist who worked meticulously and without any applause for so many years behind the camera.

History is always incomplete. No account, however thorough, can ever convey what it was to walk through the street of a town—to watch the pretty girls or the handsome men, smell the tobacco wafting from the pubs, or hear the music and laughter of a time gone by. The photographs in this book, however, perhaps come closer than any other medium to capturing the flavor of those years. The photograph has been said to "take the fingerprints of reality" and while each shot was carefully set up and manipulated by French, who was a perfectionist, it is possible to see in them how everyday life was lived and breathed when our great-grandparents were young. It is also possible to see that, in spite of a written history that tells of a century filled with misery, Ireland's incredible beauty was untouched, her cities were bustling, and her more fortunate inhabitants enjoyed a measure of happiness and luxury. In Lawrence's treasured 40,000 photographs, it is possible to see a society that has now passed away and is all but forgotten.

Left: This photograph of fair day in Tipperary shows the cattle market which still takes place on Wednesdays and Fridays and is as busy now as it was back in the 19th century.

LISTOWEL ROSCOMMON TRIPPERARY DOWNPATRICK NEWTOWNARDS BUNCRANA BALLYSHANNON KELLS TRIM NAAS DUBLIN BRAY GALWAY ATHLONE LONGFORD BELFAST LONDONDERRY DUNDALK CORK WATERFORD CARLOW WEXFORD KILKENNY LIMERICK COLERAINE BALLYMENA KILLARNEY LOUGHREA BIRR MULLINGAR TRALEE ENNIS ARKLOW DROGHEDA CARRICK-ON-SHANNON SLIGO BALLINA LURGAN ARMAGH KILDARE TEMPLEMORE BANTRY SKIBBEREEN CLONAKILTY WESTPORT LISTOWEL ROSCOMMON TRIPPERARY DOWNPATRICK NEWTOWNARDS BUNCRANA DUNDALK CORK WATERFORD CARLOW WEXFORD KILKENNY LIMERICK COLERAINE BALLYMENA KILLARNEY LOUGHREA BIRR MULLINGAR TRALEE ENNIS ARKLOW DROGHEDA

TOWNS & CITIES

Historically, the Irish have never been particularly keen on the idea of living in towns and cities. From the earliest days of the Viking invasions and before, most of the people have preferred to live off the land, with only a few congregating in the early centers for trade along the coast such as existed at Dublin, Wexford, Waterford, and Limerick. When the Norman conquerors invaded, they built fortifications over most of the country as they had elsewhere. These locations grew to become small beacons of urban life but most of the population remained in the countryside.

It was not until the 17th century that urban development properly began—extremely late in Ireland's history. At that time plantations were awarded to British planters and the native Irish farmers were dispossessed. Towns were seen as essential centers of government in the wild Irish countryside and many new ones were built, while other derelict and forgotten towns such as Armagh were repopulated. The building work continued throughout the 18th century and was especially rapid from about 1750 onward, as the landlords and middle classes became more and more prosperous and demanded residences that reflected their status. New squares were laid out and grand and elegant buildings in the Classical style were erected in many of Ireland's old cities during this period but the center of the development work was in Dublin, which became an extremely dignified city within a relatively short space of time. However, with the Act of

Left: A traditional shillelagh maker sells his wares on the streets of Killarney, Co. Kerry.

Right: A view of Limerick, the regional capital of Co. Limerick, from across the River Shannon. The city was redeveloped during the 18th century and can boast nearly as much grand classical architecture as Dublin. Its position on the river ensured that it was a thriving trade center during the 19th century.

Far left: Davy Stephens was a Dublin street vendor who sold magazines and periodicals to passers-by. At the bottom of the picture, by Stephens' foot, the magazine called "Pick Me Up" looks as though it has been illustrated with a Lawrence photograph.

Left: This dapper gent has not been named but his clothes are a good example of the traditional Irish dress by the 19th century. Knee breeches were common, as they had been for over a century, and the "trusty" coat was generally worn in cold weather. Hats were less necessary and so were not widely worn but as in any time dress was mostly dependent on how much the wearer could afford. Pipe smoking was a very common habit among both men and women and tobacco processing took place at a number of locations including Dublin, Dundalk, Belfast, and Ballymena. Indeed, tobacco was one of Ireland's few successful 19th century exports.

Union, Dublin was no longer a hub of government and the building work all but ceased. The trends in the capital were generally true for the whole of the country and while there were, of course, a number of great works of architecture built after 1801, the most prevalent architectural style throughout urban Ireland is the Classical. Notable exceptions—such as the beautiful Catholic cathedral at Killarney and the church of Saint Peter and Saint Paul in Cork—are among the relatively few buildings in Ireland that display the shift from Classical to the Gothic Revival of the Romantic period that was popular around Europe.

Nevertheless, while Irish cities were being transformed the majority of the Irish people stayed stubbornly rural and continued with a lifestyle that remained all but unchanged by the momentous events and technological marvels that were having so great an effect elsewhere. Those forced by poverty to move into the cities in the hope of earning a wage created the growth of slum areas, as even in Belfast there was not enough work available to accommodate all the potential labor force. By the middle of the 19th century, less than 20 per cent of the people of Ireland lived in towns and unlike the rest of Europe, which was experiencing the urgent growth of industrialization, Ireland, for the most part, continued to rely on agriculture. Irish towns and cities of the 19th

Right: Only Belfast was a hub of manufactiring industry that could rival England's great manufacturing towns. This photograph was taken in Ewart's factory, Belfast and shows women weft-winding on linen mills.

Below right: Trams and horses on Belfast High Street. The city's name derives from the Gaelic *Beál Feirste* meaning "mouth of the sandy ford". The clock tower visible at the end of the street is the Albert Memorial clock tower, built following Prince Albert's death in 1861. Belfast erected many monuments and dedicated streets to Queen Victoria after her visit in 1849.

Below: Members of the local fishing fleet and their families pose on the quayside at Ardglass Co. Down.

SHOP St. GALWAY, 5043. W.L.

Far left: Galway's winding streets have been growing since it was a tiny fishing village in the days of the Normans. Over the years it developed into one of Ireland's most attractive and busy cities, with the university attracting a very bohemian crowd and its position on the east coast making it a desirable port for merchants. At its height it was a center for the trade in spices from the East and wines from Spain and Portugal.

Left: The Queen's College (Ireland) Act of 1845 provided for the establishment by the government of colleges at Cork, Galway, and Belfast, to provide higher education on a non-denominational basis. Queen's College Galway opened in 1849 and most of its students were Catholics. This picture was taken in the 1860/70s.

century fell into two categories—those that existed as a focus for the surrounding agricultural or fishing activity, and the few large coastal ports such as Dublin, Cork, Waterford, and Limerick that attracted trade. The single exception to this was Belfast, which alone in the photographic records has the appearance of a bustling industrial metropolis. By the middle of the 19th century Belfast already had a burgeoning shipbuilding industry and this would expand for over a century (it is still going strong to this day). Indeed some of the most famous ships ever to be launched—including Titanic— were constructed in the huge yards on the shores of the Belfast Lough that dominated the skyline of the city by the turn of the century. Belfast was also a center for the cotton trade and had a thriving linen trade: altogether it was a typically prosperous Victorian industrial city.

Ireland's cities, while not as thrusting and dynamic as those elsewhere in Europe, had a great intellectual life during this period. Due to the Act of Union, there were many men who bent their energies toward politics and struggled toward home rule. The universities of Dublin, Cork, Galway, and Belfast were also well-regarded and fostered the academic brilliance of such alumni as Sir William Rowan Hamilton (1805–65), one of the greatest mathematicians of the age, as well as many of the exceptional literary talents of the period. Men such as the celebrated poets Thomas Moore (1779–1852) and Samuel Ferguson (1810–86) were busy re-establishing the place of Irish culture at the beginning of the century, paving the way for an Irish literary explosion and greatly influencing the following generation of writers. Moore was the most popular Irish writer of his time and became famous (and rich) by exploiting the commonly held sentimental view of Ireland in his poems and songs—such as the ten-volume *Selection of Irish Melodies*. Ferguson was an antiquarian and poet from Belfast, and his poems rediscovered many of the ancient Celtic heroes— Cuchulain, Dierdre, Diarmid, and Queen Maeve—that would become the stock-in-trade of later writers such as W. B. Yeats (1865–1939), James Joyce (1882–1941), and J. M. Synge (1871–1909). But there was more to Irish artistic life than litera- ture, with interesting developments and talented artists in the fields of music and visual arts coming to the fore in this period.

Despite the comparative vigor of the cities, the majority of smaller communities throughout Ireland were sleepy market towns, too small to sustain any kind of cultural life and geared specifically to agricultural requirements. Architecture in these towns would typically be much more functional than in the cities; generally the only buildings of architectural note were likely to be the residence of the local landlord and the local church. The larger towns would be built around a central square, while the smaller settlements would usually comprise of a single high street, which would have a church and a school. Few of them had populations that exceeded 5,000 people, and most would have had only a few small shops and an inn or two. The height of excitement was market day, when farmers would congregate

Right: Fair days were important events when farmers and merchants from miles around would come into town to exchange goods. In many cases the market was accompanied by dancing and festivities. This photograph shows Bantry Bay in West Cork, a well-known market and fishing town. The town is also famous for being the point where a French fleet, sailing to aid an Irish uprising in 1798, was dispersed by a storm.

FAIR DAY. BANTRY. CO. CORK. 8798. W.L.

ENNISTYMON FALLS. CO. CLARE. 4137. W.L.

in town to buy or sell livestock and other goods. As agriculture was Ireland's biggest industry by far, during fertile years market days could be extremely busy, noisy affairs and would often be accompanied by music and dances. One particularly popular craze throughout the 1800s was the cake dance. A cake was posted on a stand in the middle of a dance floor as the prize at a spirited hooley. It went, of course, to the best dancer.

However, as the century progressed, even these provincial municipalities were caught up in the tide of progress. Many of the later photographs in the Lawrence collection show townspeople looking on in bewilderment as a motor car is driven down the muddy high street, rutted from the passage of so many horses and carts. These pictures can perhaps be seen as the symbolic ending of a way of life: before long radio, television, and all the other paraphernalia of modern life would have a dramatic effect on the traditional Irish lifestyle.

Left: The town of Ennistymon, Co. Clare lies on the River Inagh with its famous rapids just beside the town. The waters are famed for trout and salmon fishing.

Below: Kilkenny, renowned for its beauty, is officially a city (thanks to St. Canice's Cathedral) although it is smaller than many other Irish towns. Situated by a bend in the River Nore it is set in particularly lovely countryside and was settled by the Normans—the area still features many Norman and medieval ruins. Like most towns of any size in the 19th century it was a busy market center and it also supported a small brewing industry. Predominatly classical Georgian in appearance, the facade hides a wealth of older features.

MAIN St. KILKENNY. 4829. W.L.

WATERFALLS THE DARKLE MOUNTAINS LOUGHS IRISH SEA BOGS THE DINGLE RIVERS DONEGAL BAY LOUGH NEATH RIVER SHANNON MACGILLYDUDDY'S REEKSHIGH CROSSES MEDIEVAL RUINS MONASTERY GLENCAR SLIEVEARDAGH HILLS LOUGH ENNELL BANTRY BAY GIANT'S CAUSEWAY DRUMLINS CAIRNS CASTLES CLONMACNOISE MELLIFONT ABBEY ISLANDS MISTS GREEN WATER-FALLS THE DARKLE MOUNTAINS LOUGHS IRISH SEA BOGS THE DINGLE RIVERS DONEGAL BAY LOUGH NEATH RIVER SHANNON MACGILLYDUDDY'S REEKSHIGH CROSSES MEDIEVAL RUINS MONASTERY GLENCAR SLIEVEARDAGH HILLS LOUGH ENNELL BANTRY BAY GIANT'S CAUSEWAY DRUMLINS CAIRNS CASTLES CLONMACNOISE MELLIFONT ABBEY ISLANDS MISTS GREEN

LANDSCAPES

Even the most staunch city-dweller could not help but be moved by the Irish countryside. From the craggy, barren hills around Mount Carrauntoohil, Ireland's highest mountain, in County Kerry, to the serene Glencar Lough fed by the waterfall of the Differeen River in County Sligo, the Emerald Isle is justly famous for the awe-inspiring beauty of its natural assets. The country's affectionate nickname is well earned, for the bounty of lush green vegetation is everywhere, giving the landscape the appearance of great fertility and supporting a bewildering variety of flora and fauna. Dotted among this beautiful scenery are stone walls, grand old castles, ancient remains, and rural cottages that lend a distinctive character to a countryside that has long beguiled and inspired poets. The following lines from Synge's *Prelude* are typical of the many verses that praise the tranquillity and sublime charm of Ireland's landscape.

Left: Fishing at Glenmacnass, Co. Wicklow.

Right: A group of Glencar locals pose in front of their cottages while a little girl looks on. The poet W.B. Yeats spent much of his childhood in this part of the country and as an adult returned to it often. One of his most famous poems *The Stolen Child*, describes the landscape perfectly:

Where the wandering water gushes
From the hills above Glen-Car,
In pools among the rushes,
That scarce could bathe a star,
We seek for slumbering trout,
And whispering in their ears;
We give them evil dreams,
Leaning softly out
From ferns that drop their tears
Of dew on the young streams.

Overleaf: The spectacular view over Lough Dan in Co. Wicklow, due south of Dublin.

Still south I went and west and south again,
Through Wicklow from the morning till the night,
And far from cities, and the sights of men,
Lived with the sunshine, and the moon's delight.

I knew the stars, the flowers, and the birds,
The grey and wintry sides of many glens,
And did but half remember human words,
In converse with the mountains, moors, and fens.

The country is made up of broken ring of hills and mountains that provide a dramatic 3,000-mile coastline of mighty cliffs, and these surround a lowland area. The entire island is liberally strewn with lakes, rivers, and streams, as well as peat bogs such as the Bog of Allan in County Offaly that provided rural folk with an ample fuel supply. To the west the coastline is almost as indented as the fjords of Norway, a characteristic that means no matter where you stand in Ireland, you are never further 70 miles from the coast. This physical geography, as well as its position on the edge of the Atlantic (where the Gulf Stream flows), has

ensured that Ireland enjoys a gentle and mild, if rather moist climate which contributes to the abundance of plant and wildlife.

The fact that Ireland was endowed with such a wealth of natural beauty was not overlooked by the 19th century tourist. Particularly in the Victorian era, travel was becoming increasingly popular and affordable, as the wealth of the Empire swelled the affluent middle classes of mainland Britain. The tourist industry was also becoming ever more organized and sophisticated with hotels, rail companies, and tour operators all seeing the opportunity to make profits. And with Ireland being

Far left: A local woman sells lemonade and ginger beer to tourists on the road to Glengarriff, a popular destination for Victorian tourists. Situated in West Cork it benefits from a particularly mild climate due to the proximity of the Gulf Stream and the sheltering hills around it. The visitors would sail from England to Bantry and then take a wagon up this road to their destination.

Left: A party of picnickers finds a pleasant spot to lunch on the shores of Upper Lake, Killarney.

Page 45: Navan lies at the confluence of the rivers Boyne and Blackwater. It is famous as the birthplace of the inventor of the internationally used wind-strength scale, Sir Francis Beaufort.

so close, it was a popular destination for a growing number of sightseers eager to experience the delights of the Emerald Isle's rural splendour for themselves.

The photographs in the Lawrence collection clearly reflect this increased tourist activity. Many earlier scenes show wagon loads of people stopping outside picturesque inns for refreshments, while nearer the end of the century charabancs and motor cars filled with happy travelers can often be seen. The beaches, too, were popular with visitors. Ireland is blessed with many fine sandy shores that, on a fine day, rival any in Europe. French's ubiquitous camera recorded crowded bathing beaches (separate spots for men and women, of course), quaint bathing machines that protected a bather's modesty until they were ready to take the plunge, and children at play in the surf. Alongside the holidaymakers can be seen the more traditional means of making a living from the sea—fishermen sailing the same kind of vessels as their fathers and grandfathers before them.

The visitors also came to see the established tourist spots. French took a series of photographs of very grave looking Victorians kissing the Blarney Stone at Blarney Castle (an act which is said to confer the gift of a silver tongue on the kisser). His pictures also show uncomfortably dressed walkers inspecting the impressive basalt stacks of the Giant's Causeway in County Antrim, while old women sit among the stones with baskets of goods to sell to the tourists. Elsewhere his camera captured elegant women touring castles or sitting beneath trees sketching, picnic parties, and locals outside their cottages hoping to make a little money by selling lemonade and ginger beer to passing travelers.

However, French's scenes are, for the most part, absent of tourist activity and it is in these photographs that the utter serenity of the Irish countryside can be sensed. Whatever part of the landscape he was photographing, French went about his job with the skill and care of a master craftsman. Again and again he produced shots that were beautifully structured and as sharp as was possible with the early dry plate camera that was the cutting edge of technology in the latter stages of the 19th century. He seems to have been particularly fond of photographing waterfalls, the slow shutter speed of his camera giving an impression of rapidly moving water which was an excellent contrast to the sharply focused vegetation that often surrounded the falls. French also visited many of Ireland's 800 lakes and the images of these again show his artistic skill. He always chose his position with extreme care, taking many hours to find the perfect view: his landscapes invariably show perfect vistas of mountains sweeping down to the still, calm waters of a lough. Occasionally, French would show a single fishing boat in the picture, and this inclusion would somehow deepen the feeling of tranquillity. In other pictures he captures the ancient history of Ireland by placing in the foreground some of the myriad monuments and carvings that abound in the country's landscape. At the time he was taking these photographs there was a great resurgence of national pride in, and awareness of, Irish history. It is more than likely that French was aware of this as he traveled the country looking for scenes that would appeal to the public as typically Irish.

French was not a documentary photographer, however; his photographs were taken for purely commercial reasons—it was his job to keep Lawrence's emporium stocked with enough fresh photography to satisfy the insatiable demand for new images. Not only were these sold to tourists, but they were also used in advertising, to decorate train carriages, and adorned the walls of pubs, hotels, and inns. By the end of the 19th century it was impossible to go anywhere without seeing a Lawrence scene of Ireland.

BOYNE BRIDGE. NAVAN. CO. MEATH. 7774. W.L.

OLD MILL. BALLYCASTLE. 7025. W.L.

Far left: A young girl sits with her arm around a small child at the Old Mill, Ballycastle. French had a talent for making his photographs look very natural despite the fact that he put a lot of thought into constructing the scene. So meticulous was he that it is likely that he actually arranged the girl's hat and hair before taking the picture.

Left: A group of women sit in the Wishing Chair at the Giant's Causeway, Co. Antrim, with baskets full of souvenirs to sell to the tourists; even in the 19th century this was a famous, often-visited Irish landmark.

WHEAT BARLEY OATS SUGAR BEET POTATOES CEREALS MARKET-GARDENING LIVESTOCK BREEDING CATTLE SHEEP DAIRY FISHERIES PEAT LINEN WEAVING SHIPBUILDING ENGINEERING CARPET-MAKING FURNITURE CLOTHING COBBLING TOURISM LACE-MAKING EMBROIDERY BOAT BUILDING NET-MAKING FARMING SMITHING CURING WEAVING SPINNING WHEAT BARLEY OATS WHEAT BARLEY OATS SUGAR BEET POTATOES CEREALS MARKET-GARDENING LIVESTOCK BREEDING CATTLE SHEEP DAIRY FISHERIES PEAT LINEN WEAVING SHIPBUILDING ENGINEERING CARPET-MAKING FURNITURE CLOTHING COBBLING TOURISM LACE-MAKING EMBROIDERY BOAT BREEDING CATTLE SHEEP DAIRY FISHERIES PEAT LINEN WEAVING SHIPBUILDING ENGINEERING

INDUSTRY & AGRICULTURE

The scales of Ireland's commercial activities were tipped heavily toward agriculture during 19th century, so much so that the only manufacturing town of any international significance during the period was Belfast. At first successful with its linen industry, it was shipbuilding and engineering that boosted the region's economy as the century progressed. Belfast was not a particularly attractive city, having much in common with the industrial towns of the mainland, with their "dark Satanic mills." Belfast shipyards were among the best and most modern in the world and gave the city an impressive, if brutal, skyline by the end of the century.

The shipbuilding industry's fortunes rose following the American Revolution, which saw to it that the British Empire no longer had access to the great American shipyards of the East Coast, and by 1820 builders of traditional sailing ships were firmly entrenched around the Belfast Lough. In that year production took a revolutionary turn when the enterprising partnership of Ritchie and McLaine launched the 115ft Belfast. This ship, small by today's standards, was one of the first major steam vessels built by a British yard, and the forerunner of a long line of famous vessels whose ghosts now haunt Belfast Lough.

Not surprisingly, this heavily Protestant area rapidly developed a very different political and economic outlook to the rest of Ireland. Economically, the British connection was vital to its

Left: Ardglass fishing boats returning to harbor. Fishing has long been an important part of the Irish economy and there were many fishing ports around the coast.

Right: Women hand-making carpets at a factory in Killybegs, Co. Donegal.

Overleaf: An early side-wheel steam boat under construction in a Belfast shipyard. In the background can be seen masted ships as well as a ship with both masts and a steam funnel. This indicates that the photograph was taken around 1870s when the crossover from sail to steam was underway. Nervous shipowners were unwilling to trust to the new technology of steam power at first and insisted that their ships were equipped with both forms of power. The small boat in the picture was probably used as a ferry for short runs.

well being, and this reinforced its increasingly strident Protestantism and Unionism. Thus the one major Irish industrial city was not an attractive option for most Catholic Irishmen, especially as Catholics were severely discriminated against in its factories and shipyards.

With Belfast as the industrialized heart of Ireland, the rest of the country was generally involved in the production, preparation, and trade in foodstuffs. Dublin, Cork, and Londonderry were all busy trading ports and had the usual businesses that were a part and parcel of any city—news publishing, education, shops and trade, etc. There was also, as could be expected, a lively distilling and brewing industry (by the 19th century Guinness was the largest brewery in the world and became the first to go public), but the economy was firmly based on agriculture. While the rest of Europe surged ahead, Ireland, due to its unique political problems, dragged its heels in the race to industrialize.

The consequence of this was, of course, that the country was for the most part extremely poor. What wealth that existed was concentrated in the Protestant land-owning classes, many of who exacted exorbitant rents from their tenant farmers while living in luxury in England. The Catholic majority was left to scrape a living as best it could. Farming was the most widespread activity, but fishing off Ireland's abundantly stocked coasts also occupied thousands of fishermen while others worked at cleaning and curing the catch. Small cottage industries such as spinning, lace-making, weaving, and basket-making also allowed some to earn a small amount of money.

While farmers elsewhere found their work being made easier by the advances of the Agricultural Revolution, farming in Ireland generally continued in very the same manner as it had done for centuries. The work was carried out by hand, using simple implements such as the hoe and the scythe, and was backbreaking. French's photographs of the Irish at work in the fields show both men and women toiling equally hard—there was little room for the niceties of Victorian etiquette concerning women. Rural life was often depicted as a idyllic by the writers of the time, but the truth was that it was an exhausting existence and the Irish tenant farmers were constantly in fear of failing harvests which meant starvation and eviction.

Famine forced many starving people to seek shelter in Ireland's new workhouses or—especially during the Great Famine of 1845–49—on civil construction programs such as new road building. Workers were granted barely adequate food and shelter; unsurprisingly, many turned to begging on the roads as a preferable alternative to being slowly worked to death. After the Great Famine, further problems were caused by the move away from arable farming. New landlords, often financial speculators with no agricultural background or personal interest in the land and people, were much more interested in raising cattle, and poor farmers without the capital to purchase the expensive beasts were often evicted to make way for those who could.

Those lucky enough to live by the coast were not as badly affected by the famine as the people of the interior lowlands. The seas around Ireland are particularly rich in marine life (many parts of coastal Ireland are famous for their seafood dishes) and as well as fishing the sea provided others with work. Boat-makers practiced their craft much as their forefathers had done, creating the traditional "currachs" (coracles) that glided easily over the waters. A more unusual way of making a living from the ocean was that of burning seaweed (called kelp). This was used in bleaching fabrics and glass manufacturing, and a familiar sight along the seashores would be men and women with pitchforks loading seaweed into barrows and wagons to be burned nearby.

Another rural industry was peat cutting. Ireland has few forests and no coal, but peat bogs are abundant in the lowland

FISH & VEGATABLE WOMEN. 2704. W.L.

Far left: Farming was backbreaking work for both sexes for most of the year, but especially around harvest time. Wheat was widely grown in Ireland during the 19th century but most of the harvest would have been taken by the landlord, leaving the farmers with the potato crop for their own food.

Left: These two women are on their way to market carrying an astonishing load of vegetables.

areas. Peat was the only cheap source of fuel for the majority of the people who could not afford to pay inflated prices for imported coal. When it burns it gives off a smoky, distinctively red blaze, and it is still widely used on Irish fires today. Back then it was cut by hand and hauled by cart to its destination—a business that allowed many families to earn a scant living.

The only part of the population that did not suffer to any extent during the 19th century was the Protestant ruling classes. As they owned the land and businesses and maintained a vice-like grip on local administration, the judiciary, the military, and the professions, it was easy for them to maintain their privileged lives at the expense of the majority. Indeed, many businesses flourished during the period, not least Lawrence's photographic studio and fancy goods emporium in Dublin—an indication that there was money in Dublin to be spent on luxuries. This was despite the fact that Irish trade was legislated against by the British Parliament who did not want any industrial competition from their close neighbor.

Far left: This photograph, taken in Leenane, Co. Galway, shows the traditional process of turning raw wool into fabric. The wool from the sheep was "carded" between two large combs to straighten it before it was spun. The large skeins of wool that can be seen hanging up were then woven into the finished material on the loom.

Left: This family is cutting peat from a bog in the old-fashioned way before machinery took over the process. The amount of cut turf in the photograph shows how much this fuel was used in a country with no coal and very little wood.

Far left: Irish schools were not simple educational establishments but also centers of industry. In this workroom at Baltimore School, Co. Cork, children are put to work making and mending nets for the local fishing community.

Left: Fishwives at Port Magee curing the catch ready for transportation. Before refrigeration, both fish and meats were commonly salted, smoked, or dried so that they could be stored without rotting.

O'FLANNERY O'QUINN O'SHEEHAN O'QUIRKE O'CONNELL DILLON O'FLANAGAN O'DEVLIN O'KENNY O'GRADY O'SHEA McELLIGOTT O'PHELAN KENNEDY FLEMING O'CONNOR McMAHON O'SHAUGHNESSY O'DRISCOLL FAGAN DEASE NUGENT O'CONNOLLY O'DOHERTY JOYCE O'HANLEY O'MALLOY DUGAN DEMPSEY WOGAN O'HARA O'FLANNERY O'QUINN O'SHEEHAN O'QUIRKE O'CONNELL DILLON O'FLANAGAN O'DEVLIN O'KENNY O'GRADY O'SHEA NUGENT O'CONNOLLY O'DOHERTY JOYCE O'HANLEY O'MALLOY DUGAN DEMPSEY WOGAN O'HARA O'FLANNERY O'QUINN O'SHEEHAN O'QUIRKE O'FLANNERY O'QUINN O'SHEEHAN O'QUIRKE O'CONNELL DILLON O'FLANAGAN O'DEVLIN O'KENNY O'GRADY O'SHEA McELLIGOTT O'PHELAN

HOME & FAMILY

The Irish family has commonly been large, religious, and close-knit. Catholicism teaches that its followers should allow God's will to determine the size of their families, and in a largely Catholic country the consequences are obvious. Until the devastating effects of famine and emigration, Ireland's population boomed. Although the first accurate census was not taken until 1841, all evidence points to a massive increase before this, with some historians suggesting that the population doubled during the first four decades of the 19th century.

These people mostly lived cramped together in small rural cottages, with few rooms, where life would be centered on the kitchen and the fireside. Even in the years of good harvests before the Great Famine, existence would have been basic and hard at times, but the potato crops would have kept most above the subsistence level and Ireland's fruitfulness meant that her people could look forward to annual treats. At harvest time children would be sent out with pails to return loaded down with nuts and berries that would then be carefully stored or preserved to provide extra food during the lean winter months. Irish fare for the majority was plain but wholesome. Unlike most countries Ireland never really developed any haute cuisine and the meals that were put on the 19th century table would have been simple but delicious. Potatoes were used widely, of course, but with

Left: Urban areas did not see the same deprivations as rural areas. Indeed, many fled to the cities as a result of the harsh conditions in the countryside. This is Poole Street in Dublin, on washing day.

Right: Dressed up for the photographer, this is not a poor family: the horse and cart and slate roof imply a wealth and level of subsistence aspired to by many Irish men and women of the time.

THE HOUSE AT HOME 10450 W.L.

imagination. Recipes such as hot potato scones are delicious to this day, while the classic Irish Stew—originally made with mutton (lamb would have been an undreamed of luxury), potatoes (to give bulk), and onions (for flavor)—would simmer on the hearth for days with stock, meat, and vegetables tipped in to keep it topped up. This may not have provided diners with much variety but it would have been a hot, tasty, and wholesome meal in winters when food was a premium.

As mentioned before, the Irish have always seemed to feel more comfortable living in the countryside than in the towns and cities built mostly by the British invaders, yet they have always been a sociable race of people as many photographs of the time show. Music and dancing were as popular in the 19th century as they are these days when Ireland produces a disproportionate number of rock and pop stars. The Irish also had a continuing

love of legends and stories. Before the days of radio and television, evenings would be spent huddled around the fire while an elder member of the family would tell stories of fairies, spirits, mythical heroes, and magic. Sadly, this pastime is virtually dead in modern Ireland but fortunately enough of these stories were recorded in the 19th century to give an idea of the scope of Ireland's oral tradition.

This is not to suggest, however, that all of Ireland's peasantry lived in pastoral harmony. In general, the century was plagued by poverty. As it progressed and the population increased, life became meaner and the harvest, much of which was taken by the landlord, had to stretch further and further. The lack of work, when added to the growing population of the early decades, meant that already small farms were split up into ever decreasing plots that could barely feed the families that

Far left: Lawrence's caption identifies this as the inside of Conaghers Farm in County Antrim, the home of the McKinley family. There's a substantial cooking pot and a kettle on the fire, flat irons heating in front and an oil lamp on the wall: all the modern conveniences of a farmer's house of the 1880s!

Left, Below left, and Below: While the Land Act of 1881 conceded the "three Fs"—fair rent, fixity of tenure, and freedom of the tenant to sell right of occupancy—and may have put Irish landlords on the defensive, it most certainly did not stop evictions. The Lawrence collection records many such dreadful scenes as families are evicted from their homes, the walls of the cottages destroyed by the landlords' agents to prevent reoccupation. Often, as seen below, the agents needed protection provided by armed members of the Royal Irish Constabulary.

Far left: Now joined to the mainland by a bridge, Achill Island is today known as a holiday area, with wonderful beaches, what are said to be the tallest cliffs in Europe, and the historic abandoned village of Slievemore. Probably deserted by its inhabitants as a result of the Great Famine—although the arrival of a proselytizing Protestant group in 1834 may also have played its part—it is overlooked by the dramatic Slievemore mountain (672m). The village of Keel, where these fishermen posed for French's camera, is on the south coast and known for its excellent beach.

Left: The Irish travelers, many of them set on the road by the deprivations of the Great Famine, were mainly tinsmiths, earning their living by repairing metal household goods, and riding around the countryside, as here, in wagons. This photograph shows William and James, the young sons of a traveling tinsmith, with their trophy. Guess what's going in the pot tonight!

depended on them. The majority also suffered legislated oppression, having limited constitutional rights and certainly no rights over the land they occupied. So when famine struck more harshly than ever, more and more people were pushed into emigration. The promise of a richer life abroad (particularly in America) lured a flood of people away from their homeland and onto the great ships that were being built in Belfast. The promises of wealth and properity in a new land proved to be illusory in most cases however and immigrants found that life overseas was equally as hard as it had been at home. Penniless on arrival, they were forced into menial labor—if they found work at all—and the Irish would not find their feet in these distant lands for another generation or two.

Marriage for most of the rural population came later in life than anywhere else in Europe. Parents were very much involved in the process of selecting partners for their children and arranging dowries and it has been argued that this fact, rather

than any natural reticence, was the reason for their tardiness. At a time when land was scarce, many couples would have been unwilling to relinquish any to their married children or feed additional mouths; thus they tended to leave it as long as possible before giving in to the inevitable and arranging for their sons and daughters to wed. Few marriages were founded in love or romance but the prudent family would choose carefully and the system worked well for the Irish of the 19th century, allowing them to protect their own future and negotiate mutually beneficial terms with the parents of their child's betrothed.

Religion was an integral part of life for almost everyone in the British Isles during the 19th century and in the Victorian era particularly, but the Catholic Irish held their faith especially close to their hearts—perhaps because they had been so persecuted for it. For over 150 years Catholics had been imprisoned, exiled, and even killed because of their religion, and it had cost the

Far left: Children playing outside a row of fishermen's cottages. Note the half-built coracles in front—most fishermen would be adept at making their own boats and tools.

Left: This Blarney hotel lounge gives an excellent feel of Victorian provincial charm. A formidable collection of guests sits among potted palms, orchids, and arum lillies, while at the far end of the room a pair of cannon stand ready. Blarney is famous for its Scottish baronial house, the seat of the Colthirst family since the 18th century, and for the Blarney stone set in the wall of Blarney castle. (See page 68.)

wealthy Catholics their land and power. As the 19th century dawned, however, the British government slowly relaxed the discriminatory legislation and Catholics were given the right to worship freely and vote once more. Many schools and hospitals were subsequently set up and run by the Catholic religious orders such as the Patrician Brothers and the Sisters of Mercy. The only hope of any education that many of the poorer Irish children could have had, would have been under the tuition of monks, priests, and nuns. It is indicative of the place and power of the Irish Catholic church that, at the time of the mass emigration, it focused its missionary efforts on sending priests out to the new Irish communities around the world.

Ireland has a long tradition of supporting "people of the roads." From ancient times bards, poets, and latterly "poor scholars," wandered the country going from door to door and demanding hospitality in return for their services. By the mid-19th century, however, these people were mostly dispossessed

or starving victims of eviction and famine, and were beggars or tried to make a living as peddlers of cheap goods.

At the other end of the social spectrum the Protestant, aristocratic, land-owning Irish enjoyed lifestyles that were similar to those of their counterparts across the Irish Sea. The mansions of the landlord classes were as imposing as any English country seat and genteel English manners were de rigueur. A greater divide between the classes cannot be imagined. While the aristocracy lived in luxury, wore the latest fashions, were waited on hand and foot, organized shooting parties, and sent their immaculately dressed children to the finest schools, the peasantry wore rags, toiled endlessly to make ends meet, and put their unshod children to work as soon as they could stand, often without any education whatsoever. There were about 12,000 landlords in 1850 and these men owned 15 million acres between them—a huge amount of land, which made them as enormously rich as the millions of people who worked their lands were terribly poor.

Far left: Portumna is on the west bank of the Shannon in County Galway, to the north of Lough Derg, the largest of the loughs on the river. Today a center for boating holidays with a modern marina, Portumna boasts a 17th century castle, seat of the de Burgo family, and a ruined, mainly 15th century, priory. Known for its lively market, Portumna was a prosperous location in the late 19th century. This is its Roman Catholic chapel, the local priest standing proudly in front of the tower.

Left: Captioned "An ould couple" and "A Happy Pair," this couple obviously caught French's eye as much for their dress as anything else. He sports a tail coat and britches, she a long black cloak and a complicated headcovering.

HURLING GAELIC FOOTBALL HANDBALL CAMOGIE CRICKET GOLF RUGBY BRIDGE LAWN TENNIS
BADMINTON CHESS FISHING SAILING HORSE RACING SHOWJUMPING HUNTING BICYCLING
PICNICKING BOWLPLAYING WALKING BOXING MUSIC AND DANCING DRINKING HURLING
GAELIC FOOTBALL HANDBALL CAMOGIE CRICKET GOLF RUGBY BRIDGE LAWN TENNIS
HURLING GAELIC FOOTBALL HANDBALL CAMOGIE CRICKET GOLF RUGBY BRIDGE LAWN TENNIS
BADMINTON CHESS FISHING SAILING HORSE RACING SHOWJUMPING HUNTING BICYCLING
PICNICKING BOWLPLAYING WALKING BOXING MUSIC AND DANCING DRINKING HURLING
GAELIC FOOTBALL HANDBALL CAMOGIE CRICKET GOLF RUGBY BRIDGE LAWN TENNIS

PASTIMES

The Irish are very keen on sports and games of all kinds—from football to chess—and many have been part of Ireland's heritage for hundreds of years. They also have a love of taking it easy and many like nothing better than to spend the day in a good pub with a few pints of beer, some convivial company, and music in the background. Such pastimes are ingrained into Irish tradition and are as much a part of the national character as the scenery or poetry.

It is remarkable that in all French's many years of traveling around Ireland and in all the thousands of photographs that he took, not once did he see fit to record the greatest sport in the country. Hurling has been a feature of Irish life forever and it is said that many of Ireland's many mythical heroes were no strangers to the field. Indeed, it is difficult to imagine that would have reached the lofty status of hero at all if they had less than masterful with the four-foot ash caman and the fist-sized sliothar! In the 19th century the sport was only temporarily stopped by the Great Famine and the sudden mass exodus that followed. Toward the end of the century, it was as popular again as it had ever been, if not more so due to the resurgence of national pride in all things Irish that swelled during the later decades. Soon after the Gaelic Athletic Association was founded in 1884, it began the first national championships and instituted rules including the reduction of the teams to 21-a-side (there was

Left: A party on the battlements of Blarney castle watches one of their number prepare to kiss the Blarney Stone. Whether kissing it bestows the "gift of the gab" or the "ability to lie for seven years" is difficult to pinpoint. Certainly its exposed position is not for the faint-hearted.

Right: With a pint of stout at his elbow, a player starts on the *Uileann* pipes. Increasingly popular from the start of the 18th century as the Irish warpipes—*Piob mor*, Scottish-style bagpipes—fell from grace, the Uillean pipes were powered by the strength of the piper's elbow (to which a bellows was attached) rather than the capacity of his lungs. It has a greater range—two octaves—than the bagpipes and, along with the fiddle, became one of the most popular instruments of the 18th and 19th centuries.

Far left: Bicycling was a popular 19th century pastime. This view shows tricycles in Phoenix Park, Dublin, Europe's largest enclosed city park that was opened to the public in 1745.

Left: One of the most popular destinations for day trippers was the race course. Always a favorite of the Irish, horse races were attended by all classses as this photograph of Punchestown races shows. The photograph was probably taken during the visit of Edward Prince of Wales in 1868 and shows soldiers in uniform mixing with all classes of Irish society.

a time when each side could field a team of over 200 players). Since then, every year has seen a titanic struggle between brave, dextrous, and skillful teams to be the best in Ireland, though the team sizes have now been reduced even further to 15-a-side.

Hurling is not the only all-Irish sport however. Games such as Gaelic football, handball, and camogie (a similar game to hurling that is played by women) are still widely played though perhaps only bowlplaying can rival hurling in terms of age and popularity. The latter is usually played by two men who take it in turns to heave an iron ball between two points on a public road. The winner is the player to reach the finish line first, having negotiated obstacles in the road such as slopes and curves.

French did, however, take many pictures of a sport that was introduced to Ireland in the 19th century and has been beloved ever since—golf. Introduced by visitors from Scotland, at first it was played in a very irregular fashion. With no purpose-built courses available, any patch of grassland would do and French's photographs, taken all over the country, show that a huge number of middle class Irish of both sexes took to the game with a passion.

Other Irish pastimes were more sedate. Bicycling was seen as a beneficial and gentle exercise, and walking was popular too—hardly surprising in a country so blessed with natural beauty. Family picnics also took advantage of the scenery and during the 19th century it was common to see large groups picnicking in leafy glades or on village greens where they would be serenaded by bands.

Music has always been a source of great national pride and an essential part of any Irish gathering. In pubs it was tradition-ally played as a background to conversation and performers were careful not to make their songs so intrusive as to drown out the flow of talk. At dances, however, it was a different story altogether, and pipers, fiddlers, harpists, accordionists, and *bodhrán* players would strike up fast, lively tunes to encourage dancers into ever greater efforts. It is almost impossible to tell what the rural musicians of the 19th century would have sound-ed like. The great Irish oral tradition meant that songs had been passed down from generation to generation but there was also a custom of improvisation that meant that songs changed time and time again over the years, never remaining static. While

IRISH FIDDLER 6621 W.L.

Previous page: Golfers at Greystones, Co. Wicklow, one of over 300 golf courses in Ireland.

Far left: The park at Warrenpoint, Co. Down. Situated on Carlingford Lough on the way to Newry, at the western edge of the Mountains of Mourne, Warrenport was a bustling town in the 19th century. Here a crowd listens to a pianist playing in the park bandstand.

Left: The fiddler occupies a special place in Irish music, an essential part of today's traditional bands. There are many styles of playing—from the aggressive bowed staccato of Donegal to the fingering skills of County Clare. W. B. Yeats says in his "The Fiddler of Dooney":

For the good are always the merry,
Save by an evil chance,
And the merry love the fiddle,
And the merry love to dance.

Left: A shooting party under the imposing Cathedral Cliff, Achill Island. Ireland has always been renowned for its rural sports.

there was some effort made in the 19th century to record some of these song, the collectors were rarely able to understand Gaelic and usually tried to interpret them in terms of European classical music. Even the *Irish Melodies* of Thomas Moore owe more to classical traditions than they do to real Irish folk music of the time, though they were inspired by old tunes. Nevertheless it can be said with certainty that music for the 19th century Irish was as much about meeting up and having fun as it remains for their modern descendants.

Music and dancing are thoroughly intertwined in Irish history and like the music, the dance was originally much different from the way it is now. Most people, when they think of traditional Irish dance, will immediately imagine that Riverdance is a good example. However, the 19th century dancers would have been quite bewildered by the stiff-armed steps of today's troupes. In those days the entire body was used in the jigs, reels, and hornpipes, the best dancers being those who danced themselves into a blur. The relatively recent change, with the insistent rigidity in the hands and arms, may well have been a concession to the church (at around the turn of the century) whose priests had long been unhappy at the sight of free movement during dancing. It seems that parish priests, unable to dent the popularity of dancing, insisted that arms were kept down by the sides. Dances were less abandoned this way and it appeared that the dancers were showing some self control. It also happened that dances held in front parlours and the like were so overcrowded that it made good sense to quell arm movements.

It is perhaps an indicator of the character of Irish people that during the hardship and oppression of the 19th century, and before, such simple pleasures and traditions were not lost to them but enjoyed, sometimes in secret, with each successive generation to remain as vibrant now as they were then.

Left: A picnic in Clonmacnoise, Ireland's most important monastic site, on the Shannon in County Offaly. Said to have been founded in 545 AD by St. Ciaran, it was particularly famous from the 7th century onward as a seat of learning and the burial location of the high kings of Connacht and Tara. It was attacked by the Vikings, the native Irish, the Normans, and—in 1552—the English, who plundered everything that remained. All that survives today are the ruins of two churches and the cathedral, two round towers, and a number of spectacular High Crosses, including the 9th century Cross of the Scriptures.

Overleaf: Walkers take advantage of the fresh strawberries and cream on sale at a local cottage near the strawberry beds, Dublin.